# The Beats In Denver
# A Self-Guided Tour

## Where Kerouac, Cassady and Ginsberg Hung Out

Michael Reid

For Max Reid, my superhero

# Table of Contents

## Introduction

neighbors.denverpost.com

After a night hitting the bars in Cheyenne, Wyoming, Sal Paradise [Jack Kerouac] in *On the Road* says, "I woke up with a big headache. Slim was gone – to Montana, I guess. I went outside. And there in the blue air I saw for the first time, far off, the great snowy tops of the Rocky Mountains. I took a deep breath. I had to get to Denver at once."
*On The Road*, Jack Kerouac. With an introduction by Ann Charters. Penguin edition, 1991.

Denver is one of the important Beat cities.

• Jack Kerouac, as narrator Sal Paradise in *On The Road*, visits Denver three times. In 1949, Kerouac, along with his mother, sister and brother-in-law, moved to Denver for a brief time. Kerouac talks about Denver throughout his book *Visions of Cody*.

- Neal Cassady, the inspiration for the character Dean Moriarity in *On The Road* and Cody Pomeray in *Visions of Cody*, grew up in Denver.

- Neal's wife Carolyn Cassady, who wrote *Off The Road. My Years With Cassady, Kerouac and Ginsberg*, moved to Denver in 1946 to study for her MA degree in Theater and Fine Arts at the University of Denver.

- Allen Ginsberg, author of *Howl and Other Poems*, lived in Denver and Boulder. Ginsberg and Anne Waldman founded the Jack Kerouac School of Disembodied Poetics at the Naropa Institute in Boulder.

- William S. Burroughs, author of *Naked Lunch*, lived in Boulder for a time and taught at the Naropa Institute.

- Other Beats and Beat friends lived in or visited Denver and Boulder including Allan Temko, Hal Chase, Al Hinkle, Ed White, Gregory Corso and Phillip Whalen.

You can still walk the Denver streets that Cassady and Kerouac did. Some of the buildings are gone, but many are still there. Most importantly, their words have lasted and through these you can see, as you follow their paths, the city they saw.

This book contains passages from works by Kerouac, Cassady and Ginsberg describing where they hung out in Denver. As you visit the places, read what they wrote and see if you can feel something of what they did.

We have tired to be as comprehensive as possible in showing Kerouac, Cassady and Ginsberg sites. No book presents as many Beat places as this one. A number of sites are featured here for the first time. The tours are designed to get you from place to place in an orderly and expeditious fashion. Follow the step-by-step directions or plug the addresses into your GPS. Have fun.

9

**Timeline - Jack Kerouac** in Denver
(born March 12, 1922 in Lowell, Massachusetts)

"Kerouac by Palumbo" by Tom Palumbo from New York, NY, USA - Jack Kerouac. Licensed under CC BY-SA 2.0 via Wikimedia Commons -

- Kerouac visited Denver four times.

- July 19,1947. Age 25, Kerouac leaves New York on his first trip across the country. His travels will result in *On The Road*. On the way to San Francisco, he makes a stop in Denver. He is in Denver about a week.

- May – July 1949. Kerouac moves to Denver and lives in a house in the suburb of Westwood (now part of Lakewood, Colorado). He becomes involved with a neighbor woman and visits Lakewood Amusement Park with her and her son. His mother, sister and brother-in-law move to Westwood shortly thereafter, but his mother leaves within a month. He wanders through Denver's "Negrotown" and watches a softball game (described in *On The Road* and in *Visions of Cody*).

- From Denver, he leaves for San Francisco and visits Neal Cassady. Carolyn Cassady kicks them out of the house and they get a ride-share car to Denver. They stay for a few days with one of Jack's former neighbors in Westwood and then leave for the East Coast.

- June 1950. Kerouac's publisher, Harcourt Brace, pays for a book-signing trip to Denver. Jack travels to Denver by bus and parties non-stop with Ed White and a kid just out of reform school whom he met on the bus. Neal Cassady, who has been in New York parking cars, shows up and drives Jack to Mexico City.

- October 21, 1969. Dies in St. Petersburg, Florida of internal bleeding caused by cirrhosis, age 47. He is buried in Edson Cemetery, Lowell, Massachusetts.

act.mtv.com

**Timeline -- Neal Cassady** in Denver
(born February 8, 1926 in Salt Lake City)

Neal Cassady, in custody but still smiling

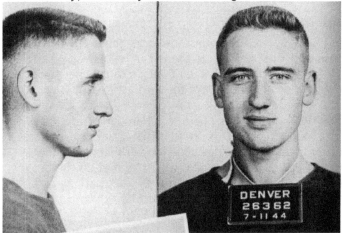

Denver Police Department photo

- 1926. Cassady's family moves to Denver from Salt Lake.

- 1932. Age 6, Neal enrolls in Ebert Elementary.

- By the time Cassady enrolls at Ebert, his father and mother have separated.  At first, Neal lives with his alcoholic father.  Then he spends several of his grade school years shuffling between his parents, staying with his mother during the school year and with his father summers.

- 1936. Neal's mother dies.

- 1938. Enrolls at Cole Junior High.  Attends off and on.

- 1940.  Neal lives for about half the year in the J.K. Mullen Home For Boys in a suburb of Denver.  He steals some athletic equipment and runs away.

- 1938 – 1947. Cassady steals 500 cars by the time he is 18 (according to his own estimate). During this time, he is arrested for car theft, shoplifting, fencing stolen goods and receiving stolen goods.

- 1942. Enrolls at East High School. Attends off and on and does not graduate.

- 1944. Serves eleven months in the Colorado State Reformatory at Buena Vista.

- 1945. Marries sixteen-year-old LuAnne Henderson.

- 1946 – 1947. At age 20, Neal travels to New York City with LuAnne. Cassady meets Kerouac and Ginsberg. Returns to Denver in March 1947.

- 1947. Jack Kerouac, on his first trip to Denver, sees Neal briefly.

- 1947. Meets Carolyn Robinson, a graduate student at the University of Denver. They marry in 1948.

- 1948 until his death. Cassady lives mostly in California. He occasionally visits Denver for short periods.

- February 4, 1968. After a night of partying, dies of exposure in San Miguel de Allende, Guanajuato, Mexico (just a year before Jack Kerouac dies). Age 41. His body was cremated.

**Timeline - Allen Ginsberg** in Denver and Boulder
(born June 3, 1926 in Newark, New Jersey)

praler.org

- Summer 1947. Comes to Denver to continue an affair with Neal Cassady that started in New York City. Lives in a basement apartment on Grant Street. Works as a night janitor at the Daniels & Fisher Department store.

- Writes poems called the *Denver Doldrums*, in part because Cassady is resistant to continue their affair. At the end of July 1947, Ginsberg leaves Denver and returns to New York City.

- 1972. Writes *The Visions of the Great Remember*, his farewell to Cassady and Kerouac and his thoughts on reading *Visions of Cody*. He talks extensively about Denver in *Great Remember*.

- 1974. Ginsberg and Anne Waldman start the Jack Kerouac School of Disembodied Poetics at the Naropa Institute in Boulder (now Naropa University).

- From 1974 until his death in 1997, Ginsberg teaches at the Kerouac School.

- 1982. Ginsberg and the Kerouac School host the 25th anniversary celebration of the publication of *On The Road*. Many of the Beats come to Boulder for the event.

- 1993. The Allen Ginsberg Library, located on the Naropa campus, is dedicated.

- Dies April 5, 1997 of from diabetes, hepatitis and liver cancer in New York City, age 70. He was cremated. Ashes are buried in the Gomel Chesed Cemetery in Newark, New Jersey as well as the Shambala Mountain Center in Red Feather Lakes, Colorado.

**What was happening in 1947? (Kerouac's first trip to Denver)**

Rocky Mountain News

- Aliens flew across the Denver skies (according to a front-page headline in the *Rocky Mountain News*).

- Lots of aliens were around in 1947. The Roswell UFO incident happened that year.

- Red Rocks Amphitheater had its first regular concert season.

- Television premiers: Howdy Doody and Captain Video.

- Arapahoe Basin ski area opened for its first official season.

- High grossing movies: *The Bachelor and the Bobbysoxer* with Cary Grant and Shirley Temple, *Road To Rio* with Bob Hope and Bing Crosby, *Miracle on 34th Street* with Maureen O'Hara.

- Top grossing movie stars: Bing Crosby, Betty Grable, Ingrid Bergman.

- Chuck Yeager breaks the sound barrier.

- Books: *The Diary of a Young Girl* – Anne Frank, *Goodnight Moon* – Margaret Wise Brown, *A Streetcar Named Desire* – Tennessee Williams, *Curious George Takes A Job* – H.A. Rey.

- Emily Griffith, founder of the Emily Griffith Opportunity School in Denver, and her invalid sister Florence are found dead, shot execution style, in their cabin in Boulder County, Colorado. The case was never solved.

- Jackie Robinson is the first African American to play in Major league baseball.

- At Denver's Mammoth Gardens event center, Everette Marshall defeated Ed "The Strangler" Lewis in professional wrestling.

Streetcar at 17th and Welton Streets, Denver. 1947.

electric-rly-society.org.uk

What was happening in 1949? (Kerouac's 2<sup>nd</sup> trip to Denver)

COURTESY: VOLKSWAGEN

- The first Volkswagen Beetle was sold in the U.S.A.

- African Americans were barred from eating at the Woolworth lunch counter in downtown Denver (and at all other Woolworths across the country).

- The Skoota Boats premiered at Lakeside Amusement Park.

- Highest grossing movie: *Samson and Delilah* with Hedy Lamar and Victor Mature.

- Top grossing movie stars: Bob Hope, Bing Crosby, Abbott and Costello.

- Top songs: *Ghost Riders In The Sky* -- Vaughn Monroe, *Rudolph the Red-Nosed Reindeer* – Gene Autry.

- Books: *1984* – George Orwell, *The Third Man* – Graham Greene, *Bartholomew and the Oobleck* – Dr. Seuss.

- The Lone Ranger premiers on television.

- Average cost of new house nationally $7,450. Average wages per year $2,950.00. Cost of a gallon of gas 17 cents. Average cost of a new car $1,420.00.

## Beat Bars

In *On The Road*, Sal Paradise (Kerouac) checks in at Roland Major's apartment and then, "We went out and drank in the Colfax bars." No specific Colfax bars are mentioned, but one possibility is The Squire Lounge. It and the rest of the bars listed below were open and serving drinks in 1947.

**Squire Lounge (Open 4:00 PM – 2:00 AM)**
**1800 East Colfax Avenue**

blogs.westword.com

This is a Beat bar, no question. It has been serving drinks on East Colfax since 1945 and whenever somebody compiles THE list of dive bars in Denver, it is there. Here is what Denver's weekly newspaper, *Westword*, says about the Squire.

"A whole-body condom couldn't protect even the hardiest of barflies from this cross-section of Colfax characters, but cut-rate cocktails and bargain-basement beer prices will surely help with the pain."
*Westword's Dozen Best Dive Bars in Denver*, April 2, 2013.

**Don's Club Tavern, formerly Don's Mixed Drinks (Open 2:00 PM – 2:00 AM) 723 E 6th Ave**

Here is what Don's website says. "...it is a virtual certainty that Jack Kerouac threw back drinks at Don's during one of his noteworthy Denver stretches - e.g. during the era when he wrote the epic *On The Road*."

Here is Zagat's opinion of Don's...
"It's a guaranteed good time at this deliciously divey Speer hole-in-the-wall that's been welcoming an interesting crowd with inexpensive cocktails on the stronger side since 1947; the unassuming digs – vinyl booths, wood paneling, pool, shuffleboard and an outdoor patio in back – also help along the easy drinking scene."
www.zagat.com/n/dons-club-tavern-denver

**Charlie Brown's Bar and Grill in the Colburn Hotel (Open 10:00 AM - 2:00 AM) 980 Grant St**

www.charliebrownsbarandgrill.com

Neal Cassady met his wife Carolyn in the Colburn Apartments. She was living at the Colburn and studying for her M.A. at the University of Denver. Charlie Brown's is located in the Colburn Hotel (the tower just north of Colburn Apartments), so naturally Cassady and Kerouac tipped a few here.

"There are many reasons to go to Charlie Brown's. The place has a lot of history - seventy-odd years of it. The inside bar feels like an archetypal neighborhood joint, and the patio - big, heated in winter - is one of the very few places left in this city where you can have a cigarette with your beers and still feel like you're actually inside. And then there's the kitchen, which does a decent job on a huge menu offering everything from breakfast burritos to a lobster dinner... Once favored by Jack Kerouac and Neal Cassady, Charlie's now draws one of Denver's most diverse crowds..."
www.westword.com/.../charlie-browns-bar-and-grill-20687/

## El Chapultepec (Open 11:00 AM – 2:00 AM) 1962 Market

El Chapultepec has seen some of the jazz greats – Ella Fitzgerald, Tony Bennett, Count Basie and Wynton Marsalis to name a few.

www.tripadvisor.com

"Opened in 1933, after the repeal of prohibition, El Chapultepec (or, the Pec as locals call it) started life as a Mexican Cantina. It served (and still serves) traditional Mexican fare, like tamales, burritos and the like, and they've also served cold beer and drinks since they first opened (they have the oldest original Coors account in the state).... Jerry Krantz, took it over. Jerry was a fan of jazz... [He] never charged a cover. You could come at any time and simply sit and listen to good music....

This was why Jack Kerouac and his crew spent so much time here in 1952. According to Jerry, they'd get high out in the parking lot and then slump in a booth (first one to your right when you enter) and listen to jazz. They didn't have to buy drinks to sit and listen -- Jerry tolerated them for free." *Exploring Denver's El Chapultepec*, The Huffington Post, January 23, 2014. [NOTE: Kerouac was not in Denver in 1952, so it must have been earlier.]

## The Cruise Room at The Oxford Hotel
**1600 17th St.  (Open 4:30 PM – 12:45 AM)**

www.westword.com

Kerouac and Cassady would not be caught dead in the 2015 version of the Cruise Room.  The patrons are upscale, respectable, well dressed and used to paying premium prices for martinis.  That was not always the case.  The Cruise Room opened the day after Prohibition was repealed in 1933 with an Art Deco look modeled after the lounges on the Queen Mary.  By the late 1940's, however, the Oxford Hotel and the Cruise Room were past their earlier glory years and becoming a place for transients and off-work railroad workers.  I have never read for a fact that Neal Cassady drank there, but at that time it was just the kind of bar he would have visited to bend an elbow.  So give it a walk-through at least.  Here is what Zagat has to say about the Cruise Room...

"Rated No. 1 for Atmosphere in Denver's Nightlife Survey, this sophisticated, pricey martini bar ... in LoDo's Oxford Hotel is a step back in time, where professional servers in vests serve up legendary libations in a unique, art deco space out of the roaring Prohibition era."
www.zagat.com/n/the-cruise-room-bar-denver

23

**My Brother's Bar   2376 15th St**
**(Open 11:00 AM to 2:00 AM)**

theburgerbaron.com

This is the oldest bar in Colorado.   It has been serving drinks since the 1880's.   There is no sign on the building and no website, but locals know where to find it.

Neal Cassady's brother worked here as a bartender when it was called Paul's Place.   Here is what Neal wrote to his friend Justin Brierly about Paul's Place while he was in The Colorado State Reformatory.   "At the corner or 15th and Platte Streets there's a café called Paul's Place, where my brother Jack used to be a bartender before he joined the army.   Because of this I frequented the place occasionally and have a small bill run up.   I believe I owe them about 3 or 4 dollars.   If you happen to be in that vicinity please drop in and pay it, will you?"
*Neal Cassady's Collected Letters, 1944 - 1967.*

**The Beat Bar Tour - A Driving Tour**
(Designated driver, cab or Uber)

This is a good one. You get to experience some of the great Denver bars. If you drive, **PLEASE NAME A DESIGNATED DRIVER.** Or, there are plenty of cabs in Denver and Uber is available. Here is the route some people like. You start at The Squire Lounge and end up at My Brother's Bar downtown.

1. **Squire Lounge - 1800 East Colfax.** Start at the Squire. Don't get carried away here. You have 5 bars to go.

2. **Go to Don's Club Tavern - 763 East 6th Avenue.** Directions from the Squire Lounge to Don's (it takes 5 - 10 minutes to get there from the Squire)...
   - Go WEST on Colfax Avenue toward the mountains (about 400 feet).
   - LEFT onto Gilpin Street (go .2 miles on Gilpin).
   - RIGHT onto East 13th Avenue (go .6 miles on East 13th Avenue).
   - LEFT onto Washington Street (go .8 miles on Washington Street).
   - LEFT onto 6th Avenue. Destination is on the left - 723 East 6th Avenue.

3. **Go to Charlie Brown's Bar and Grill in The Colburn Hotel - 980 Grant Street.** Directions from Don's Club Tavern to Charlie Brown's (5 - 10 minutes travel time)...
   - On 6th Avenue, go east toward Clarkson (only about 150 feet to your next turn).
   - LEFT onto Clarkson (go 1 block to 7th Avenue).
   - LEFT on 7th Avenue (go 4 blocks to Logan).
   - RIGHT onto Logan Street (go .4 miles on Logan).
   - LEFT onto East 10th Avenue (go about 375 feet on East 130h Avenue).
   - LEFT onto Grant Street . Destination is on the left - 980 Grant Street.

4. **Go to El Chapultepec - 1962 Market Street.**
   Directions from Charlie Brown's to El Chapultepec (10 - 15 minutes travel time)...
   - Take Grant Street south toward 9th Avenue (1 block).
   - RIGHT on 9th Avenue (go 1 block to Sherman).
   - RIGHT on Sherman (go 1 block to 10th Avenue).
   - LEFT onto 10th Avenue (go .2 miles on 10th Avenue).
   - RIGHT onto Lincoln Street (go .9 miles on Lincoln).
   - LEFT onto East 18th Avenue (go about 350 feet on East 18h Avenue.
   - RIGHT onto 18th Street . (go .7 miles on 18th Street).
   - RIGHT onto Market Street . (go .2 miles on Market Street). Destination is on the right – 1962 Market Street.

5. **Go to the Cruise Room in the Oxford Hotel - 1600 17th Street.** Directions from El Chapultepec to the Cruise Room (5 - 10 minutes travel time)...
   - LEFT on 20th Street (go 1 block to Blake).
   - LEFT on Blake (go 1 block to 19th Street).
   - RIGHT onto 19th Street (go 1 block to Wazee).
   - LEFT onto Wazee Street (go 2 blocks on Wazee.)
   - RIGHT onto 17th Street . Destination is on the left – 1600 17th Street.

6. **Go to My Brother's Bar - 2376 15th Street.** Directions from the Cruise Room to My Brother's Bar (5 - 10 minutes travel time)
   - Head northeast on 17th Street to Wynkoop (about 300 feet).
   - LEFT onto Wynkoop Street (go .9 miles on Wynkoop Street).
   - RIGHT onto 15th Street (go about .5 miles on 15th Street). Destination is on the left at 2376 15th Street.

# Jack Kerouac
# in Denver

## Jack Kerouac's first stop in Colorado - a gas station in Longmont, Colorado

Having gotten as far as Cheyenne, Wyoming, Kerouac spends a night of hard drinking at the Frontier Days celebration and in the morning gets a ride from a young man driving around the country painting.

"By the time he left me off in Longmont, Colorado, I was feeling normal again and had even started telling him about the state of my own travels. He wished me luck.

It was beautiful in Longmont. Under a tremendous old tree was a bed of green lawn-grass belonging to a gas station. I asked the attendant if I could sleep there, and he said sure; so I stretched out a wool shirt, laid my face flat on it, with an elbow out, and with one eye cocked at the snowy Rockies in the hot sun for just a moment. I fell asleep for two delicious hours, the only discomfort being an occasional Colorado ant. And here I am in Colorado! I kept thinking gleefully. Damn! damn! damn! I'm making it! And after a refreshing sleep filled with cobwebby dreams of my past life in the East I got up, washed in the station men's room, and strode off, fit and slick as a fiddle, and got me a rich thick milkshake at the roadhouse to put some freeze in my hot, tormented stomach.

Incidentally, a very beautiful Colorado gal shook me that cream; she was all smiles, too; I was grateful, it made up for last night. I said to myself, Wow! What'll Denver be like?" *On the Road*, Jack Kerouac.

The gas station used to be located on the Northeast corner of Main Street (Highway 287) and Nelson (now Ken Pratt Boulevard) in Longmont. A used car lot is on that corner as of March 2015. The station was moved about a mile south and sits on blocks at the edge of Longmont, its windows broken out and exposed to the elements.

28

The manager of the station and his family (in the picture below) lived in the apartment above the station. The "tremendous old tree" is on the far right in the picture, behind the gas station.

Views & Visions. A History of Longmont. Daily Times-Call, 2006.

The gas station today

Michael Reid 2015

Here is the door to the station bathroom.   (It is painted pink, in case you go see it.)   Kerouac freshened up in this very bathroom after his nap.

Michael Reid 2015

## Larimer Street

commons.wikipedia.org

Sal Paradise gets a ride from Longmont to Denver with a businessman who drops him off on Larimer Street. "He let me off at Larimer Street. I stumbled along with the most wicked grin of joy in the world, among the old bums and beat cowboys of Larimer Street."
*On The Road*, Jack Kerouac.

"On Larimer Street Cody's [Neal Cassady's] father was known as The Barber, occasionally working near the Greeley Hotel in a really terrible barbershop that was notable for its great unswept floor of bum's hair..."
*Visions of Cody*, Jack Kerouac.

"I saw for some reason his father on Larimer Street not caring in May – their Sunday afternoon walks hand in hand in back of great baking soda factories and along deadhead tracks and ramps, at the foot of that mighty red brick chimney a la Chirico or Chico Velasquez throwing a huge long shadow across their path in the gravel and the flat. "
*Visions of Cody*, Jack Kerouac.

31

Cody "steals another car, drives around the downtown of his old boyhood – there it all is, Larimer Street with its bright huge glitter and swarming bums, the barbershop (Gaga's), B-movie, the buffet bars; the pawnshops; and the rails, and Champa, Arapahoe; Curtis Street all red and boppy now like South Main in L.A., things have changed, grown more hep, and somehow grown more cold..."
*Visions of Cody*, Jack Kerouac.

When Kerouac arrived in Denver, Larimer Street was skid row – bums, bars, missions, pawnshops and flophouses. Today, many of the homeless still congregate in downtown, but the missions have been pushed several blocks away from the swanky shopping district around Larimer Square.

The buildings in Larimer Square give you a feeling for the Denver that Cassady and Kerouac saw. Some of the old buildings also exist between 21st and 23rd Streets on Larimer.

## Bus Station, Denver - 1730 Glenarm Place

Having just arrived in Denver, Sal calls his friend Chad King to pick him up at the bus station. "He [Chad] came into the bus station wearing jeans and a big smile. I was sitting on my bag on the floor talking to the very same sailor who's been in the Cheyenne bus station with me..." *On The Road*, Jack Kerouac.

There were two bus stations in 1947, one for Greyhound and one for Trailways. Union Bus Depot (Trailways), built in 1936, was at 501 17$^{th}$ Street. That building is gone, replaced with a skyscraper.

The Greyhound station was at 1730 Glenarm. The building that housed the station was built in 1942 and is still there, although it serves as a parking garage now. (Picture below.)

Michael Reid 2015

## Windsor Hotel - 18<sup>th</sup> & Larimer

"The next few days I wandered around Denver. It seemed to me every bum on Larimer Street maybe was Dean Moriarity's father; Old Dean Moriarity him, the Tinsmith. I went into the Windsor Hotel, where father and son had lived and where one night was frightfully waked up by the legless man on the rollerboard who shared the room with them..." *On The Road*, Jack Kerouac.

Kerouac is confusing the Windsor with the Metropolitan (where Cassady shared a room with his father and the legless man). The Windsor, however, has its own history. By the time Kerouac wandered into the Windsor, it was a broken down flophouse. But when it was built in 1880, the Windsor was Denver's first luxury hotel.

Fifty years after it was built, the Windsor had become a transient hotel. It was, however, "the only flophouse in the world with a marble fireplace in every room." The hotel was torn down in 1960.

William Henry Jackson, picture taken sometime between 1880 and 1890

## Curtis Street

"I saw the little midget newspaper-selling woman with short legs, on the corner of Curtis and 15$^{th}$. I walked around the sad honkytonks of Curtis Street; young kids in jeans and red shirts; peanut shells, movie marquees, shooting parlors. Beyond the glittering street was darkness, and beyond the darkness the West. I had to go." *On The Road*, Jack Kerouac.

Curtis Street in the 1920's

www.pinterest.com

Curtis Street was once known as Denver's 'Theater Row'. In the photograph above, taken about 1925, there were more than a dozen vaudeville and movie houses on Curtis.

Kerouac would have seen some of these buildings as he walked down Curtis, but none exist today. Most were torn down in the 1950's and 1960's.

### Roland Major Apartment – 1475 Cherry Street

"I moved in with Roland Major in a really swank apartment that belonged to Tim Gray's folks. We each had a bedroom, and there was a kitchenette with food in the icebox, and a huge living room where Major sat in his silk dressing gown composing his latest Hemingwayan short story..." *On the Road*, Jack Kerouac.

Roland Major was Allan Temko in real life. Temko met Kerouac at Columbia when they were both undergraduates. Temko appears in *On the Road* as Roland Major, in *Book of Dreams* as Irving Minko and in *Visions of Cody* as Allen Minko. Temko went on to become a Pulitzer Prize winning architectural critic.

Below is the "swank" apartment building at 1475 Cherry Street, called Cherry Manor. It was built in 1946 so it was brand new when Kerouac stayed there. As of February 21, 2015, the building was on the market for $734,000.

Michael Reid 2015

## Central City

"We brought suits and hung them in the car windows and took off for Central City, Ray Rawlins driving, Tim Gray lounging in the back, and Babe up front. It was my first view of the interior of the Rockies. Central City is an old mining town that was once called the Richest Square Mile in the World... Only a few days ago I'd come into Denver like a bum; now I was all racked up sharp in a suit, with a beautiful well-dressed blonde on my arm, bowing to dignitaries and chatting in the lobby under the chandeliers.... The opera was Fidelio."
*On the Road*, Jack Kerouac.

The Central City Opera House

Central City, along with nearby Black Hawk, now have casino gambling and attract visitors from all over.

## Five Points - 26th Avenue and Welton

In a letter to Kerouac, Neal Cassady recommends Five Points for jazz. Letter dated July 3, 1949. "Try Five Points for bop, the Rossonian Hotel; and a couple of places across the street on Welton between 26th and 27th Sts."
*Neal Cassady Collected Letters, 1944 - 1967.* Edited by Dave Moore.

"At lilac evening I walked with every muscle aching among the lights of 27th and Welton in the Denver colored section, wishing I were a Negro, feeling that the best the white world had offered was not enough ecstasy for me, not enough life, joy, kicks, darkness, music, not enough night."
*On the Road,* Jack Kerouac.

The Five Points neighborhood is named for the five-way intersection of Washington Street, 27th Street, Welton Street and 26th Avenue. In May every year, 5 Points celebrates with its JazzFest, a free event with dozens of entertainers.

At the time Kerouac visited Five Points, it was a predominantly African American neighborhood known as the "Harlem of the West." Along Welton Street, there were dozens of bars and clubs where Billie Holiday, Duke Ellington, Nat King Cole, Miles Davis, Count Basie and others performed. The Rossonian Hotel in Five Points was known for its jazz and all the black musicians stayed there. Across the street from the Rossonian is the Cervantes Masterpiece Ballroom, formerly the Casino Cabaret where Kerouac and Cassady listened to jazz.

The Roxy, another club Kerouac and Cassady visited, is a block down at 2549 Welton Street

The Rossonian Hotel

Michael Reid 2015

Kerouac, Cassady and Ginsberg would have liked Colorado's legalization of recreational pot. They liked smoking grass (they called it "tea"). The Denver Kush Club, one of many pot dispensaries in Denver, is a few doors down from Cervantes Master Ballroom.

roadtrippers.com520

## A softball game --23rd and Welton

In *On the Road*, Kerouac describes a softball game he saw in Denver.

"Down at 23$^{rd}$ and Welton a softball game was going on under floodlights which also illuminated the gas tank.  A great eager crowd roared at every play.  The strange young heroes of all kinds, white, colored, Mexican, pure Indian, were on the field, performing with heart-breaking seriousness.  Just sandlot kids in uniform.  Never in my life as an athlete had I ever permitted myself to perform like this in front of families and girl friends and kids of the neighborhood, at night, under lights; always it had been college, big-time, soberfaced; no boyish, human joy like this.  Now it was too late.  Near me sat an old Negro who apparently watched the games every night.  Next to him was an old white bum; then a Mexican family, then some girls, some boys- all humanity, the lot.  Oh, the sadness of the lights that night!  The young pitcher looked just like Dean.  A pretty blonde in the seats looked just like Marylou.  It was the Denver Night; all I did was die.  *Down in Denver, down in Denver.  All I did was die.*"  *On The Road*, Jack Kerouac.

And here is how Kerouac describes it in *Visions of Cody*.

"...I walked in that Denver Night - but at 23$^{rd}$ and Welton or 25$^{th}$, thereabouts near the gastank and the softball field; I come in there carrying my sad thoughts and also a cup of red hot and really blood red chili; with beans; no, no beans that time; at 23$^{rd}$ and Welton the lawns of soft sweet old Denver are raggedier, it's where Negro and Mexican children play all day, their parents don't tell them to get off the lawn...

Suddenly I came to a softball game under bright floodlights, with earnest glad young athletes but amateurs rushing pell-mell on the dust to the roar of audiences made up of their admiring mothers, sisters, fathers and footman buddies, *whaling* at a ninth inning rally, throwing up dustclouds at second base, slapping doubles off the leftfield foulpole and stretching them into crazy triples only it's foul and there are groans.

... and me, in the back, sitting with an old bum whose only interest at the moment is looking over at a neighbor's sidepocket where latter's keeping an extry can of cold beer while he's opening the other with a can opener...

I look, on the street, at the intersection, cars are stopped at the red light; there's exhaust smell; across the traffic, on the rickety porches, behind lawns, the folks stretch in their evening darkness and occasionally look at the game or up at the moon and stars, and it's another summer.

So I died, I died in Denver; I said to myself, 'What's the use of being sad because your boyhood is over and you can never play softball like this...'" *Visions of Cody*, Jack Kerouac.

Sonny Lawson Field – 23$^{rd}$ & Welton – Sonny Lawson Field

www.westword.com

## Wholesale fruit at Denargo Produce Market
## 2797 Wewatta Way

In 1949, Kerouac moved to Denver for a brief time. As he says in *On the Road*, "In the spring of 1949 I had a few dollars saved from my GI education checks and I went to Denver, thinking of settling down there. I saw myself in Middle America, a patriarch. I was lonesome. Nobody was there..." *On the Road*, Jack Kerouac.

"I wandered around Curtis Street and Larimer Street, worked awhile in the wholesale fruit market where I almost got hired in 1947 – the hardest job of my life; at one point the Japanese kids and I had to move a whole boxcar a hundred feet down the rail by hand with a jack-gadget that made it move a quarter-inch with each yank. I lugged watermelon crated over the ice floor of reefers into the blazing sun, sneezing."

Denargo Market, built in 1939, had stalls for 504 produce growers. The market burnt down in a four-alarm fire.

Below, the Denargo Market in the 1940's.

www.roccosproduce.com

## 27<sup>th</sup> and Federal

In *On the Road*, Sal Paradise (Kerouac) makes a second trip to Denver, then decides to go to San Francisco to see Dean Moriarity. He meets up with Dean and they head back to Denver in a ride-share car (Kerouac's stay in SF only lasted a few days).

"It was with a great deal of silly relief that these people let us off the car at the corner of 27<sup>th</sup> and Federal. Our battered suitcases were piled on the sidewalk again, we had longer ways to go. But no matter, the road is life." *On the Road*, Jack Kerouac.

These houses are at Federal and 27<sup>th</sup> Avenue

Michael Reid 2015

## A Carnival at Alameda and Federal

blog.dowdlefolkart.com

"The cousin dropped us [Kerouac and Cassady] off at the sad lights of a carnival on Alameda Boulevard at Federal... We dug the carnival together. There were merry-go-rounds, Ferris wheels, popcorn, roulette wheels, sawdust, and hundreds of young Denver kids in jeans wandering around. Dust rose to the stars together with every sad music on earth." *On The Road*, Jack Kerouac.

"... we spent an hour walking in a carnival, Cody [Neal Cassady], for some reason, wearing jeans for the first time since Joanna days (for me), in the starry night strolling, among hobbledehoys and carrousels, the pretty lips of Mexican girls too young, the boys in the tent shrouds smoking over motorcycles, the sawdust, candy apples, apple wombs, socket machines, giraffes, hurt ladies of the circus, flap walls of Teeny Weeny shows... Cody (twenty-five blocks from my Welton and 23$^{rd}$ sorrows) is hung on the pretty four-foot Mexican midget beauty in the motel yard across the road..." *Visions of Cody*, Jack Kerouac.

There is nothing left at Alameda and Federal to remind you of the Beats.

## Stealing a softball

"Nothing happened that night; we went to sleep. Everything happened the next day.  In the afternoon Dean [Neal Cassady] and I went to downtown Denver for our various chores and to see the travel bureau for a car to New York.  On the way home in the late afternoon we started out for Oki Frankie's, up Broadway, where Dean suddenly sauntered into a sportsgoods store, calmly picked up a softball on the counter, and came out, popping it up and down in his palm.  Nobody noticed; nobody ever notices such things." *On the Road*, Jack Kerouac.

In 1949, the only sporting goods store on Broadway and close to downtown was Capitol Sporting Goods Shop at 1518 Broadway.  The old buildings in the 1500 block of Broadway are gone.

The Brown Palace Hotel, not far from where Neal stole the softball.

commons.wikimedia.org

45

**Kerouac's home in the Denver area in 1949**
**6100 West Center Avenue, Lakewood**

Kerouac lived in this house when he moved to Denver in 1949. He says he was lonely that summer. No wonder, this place is a long way from the downtown hot spots he liked to visit. It is a pretty good hike to even get to the nearest tavern.

Michael Reid 2015

## YMCA
## 25 E 16th Ave

In 1949, before he moved into the house at 6100 West Center Avenue in the Denver suburb of Westwood, Kerouac lived for a time at the downtown YMCA.

The downtown YMCA building was completed in 1907. Membership was limited to white men, so in 1924 the Association built a separate "colored" facility at 28$^{th}$ and Glenarm.

Another famous alum of the downtown YMCA is John Naismith, the man who invented basketball. Naismith was physical education director at the downtown facility while he went to medical school at the University of Colorado (obtaining his M.D. in 1898).

commons.wikimedia.org

## Denver Dry Goods Building
### 16<sup>th</sup> and California

In 1950, Kerouac's first book, *The Town and the City,* came out. Harcourt-Brace, the publisher, paid for a book-signing trip to Denver. The signing was held in the basement of the Denver Dry Goods Building.

The Denver Dry Goods building was, for a while at least, the largest department store west of Chicago and its motto was "Where Colorado Shops With Confidence." The building was converted to apartments in 1994.

Michael Reid 2015

## Elitch Gardens (the old location) and Elitch Theater
## 4655 West 37th Avenue

Jack Kerouac, Neal Cassady and other Beats went to the old Elitch Gardens to smoke "tea" (marijuana).

For more than a hundred years, Elitch Gardens was an amusement park located northwest of downtown Denver. It was a fun, family place. You could bring a picnic and sit on the grass. Parking was free. And Elitch Gardens had some great rides including the Tilt-A-Whirl, Sky Ride, Wild Mouse and Mister Twister, a wooden roller coaster. The old Elitch Gardens closed in 1994, and opened under different ownership in 1995 near downtown.

The Elitch Theater was part of the Gardens. It was the oldest summer stock theater in the United States. Although the amusement park was torn down and redeveloped, Elitch Theater has been maintained and restored. In August 2015, the theater will present its first live performances since it closed in 1991.

The old Elitch Gardens in full swing

coolrain44.wordpress.com

**Lakeside Amusement Park**
**4601 Sheridan Boulevard**

When Kerouac lived in Denver in the summer of 1949, he went with a female friend and her son to Lakeside Amusement Park. Neal Cassady also likely went to the midget auto races at Lakeside.

Lakeside Amusement Park opened in 1908 and is still operating, making it one of the oldest amusement parks in the United States. It, like the original Elitch Gardens, offers free parking and encourages visitors to bring a picnic. It is far less expensive than the current edition of Elitch Gardens in downtown Denver and has old, traditional rides and lot of rides for young children. The Park sits along Lake Rhoda where you can take a paddleboat ride.

The Wild Chipmunk roller coaster/Lakeside Amusement Park

www.themeparkreview.com

50

# Neal Cassady
## in Denver

**Colfax Elementary School**
**526 Tennyson Street, Denver, CO 80204**

In the summer of 1929, the Cassady family moved into a house on West Colfax and Stuart Street. "...little Neal, 3, played every afternoon in the schoolyard directly across the street."
*The First Third & Other Writings*, Neal Cassady.

The school is Colfax Elementary. It is still in operation and every day kids play on the same schoolyard.

The schoolyard where little Neal, age 3, played every afternoon

Michael Reid 2015

## The Metropolitan Hotel - 227 16th Street

"It was the month of my sixth birthday, and the usual fierce winter was upon the city when my Dad and I moved into the Metropolitan. This is a five-story building on the corner of 16th and Market Streets, in peril of collapse. It housed about a hundred of Denver's non-transient bums... On each of the upper floors there were some thirty-odd cubicles whose walls, failing by several feet to reach it, made the ceiling incongruously high. These sleeping cells mostly rented for ten or fifteen cents a night, except for certain superior ones that cost two-bits, and we had one of these, but we only paid a weekly rate of one dollar, because of the top-floor location and because we shared the room with a third person.

This roommate of ours slept on a sort of platform made by a plank covering a pipe elbow in the building's plumbing. Not just anyone could sleep there in comfort, for the ledge was only about three feet long. He fit in the space snugly enough; both of his legs had been amputated at the thigh many years previously. Appropriately, he was called "Shorty"... *The First Third*, Neal Cassady.

Historian Tom Noel, author of a number of excellent books on Denver and Colorado history, said the Metropolitan was "the fleabag of all fleabags." I have never seen a picture of the Metropolitan Hotel, but the Denver Public Library has a picture of the Alamo Hotel that looks like it was between 16th and 17th streets on Market. The Alamo may have been the name of the hotel before it became the Metropolitan (note in the picture below that it is only four stories; Cassady says the Metropolitan was five stories; writing from memory, however, he is not always accurate in *The First Third*).

The Alamo Hotel – 1913? - Looking from the 17th and Market. The Alamo may have preceded the Metropolitan.

The Denver Public Library, Western History Collection

### Daniels and Fisher Tower
### 1601 Arapahoe Street, Denver, CO 80202

"In the nighttime of Metropolitan squalor, we slept side by side, my Dad and I, in a bed without sheets. There happened to be no clock, so I relied on the Daniels and Fisher mammoth tower to wake me for school, which it did." *The First Third*, Neal Cassady.

The Daniels & Fisher Tower was built in 1910 as part of the Daniels & Fisher Department store. Both Neal Cassady and Allen Ginsberg worked at the department store in the summer of 1947. The Daniels and Fisher store was demolished in the early 1970's, but the tower was saved. It is 325 feet tall and was modeled after St. Mark's Bell Tower in Venice, Italy.

The tower has been developed into lofts and offices. Lanie's Clocktower Cabaret is in the basement. The top five floors belong to Clock Tower Events, a wedding and party venue. There are guided tours of the building on Saturdays.

denverinfill.com

**Cassady's route from the Metropolitan Hotel to Ebert Elementary**
As described in *The First Third & Other Writings*, Neal Cassady.

"Leaving the Metropolitan for school each day, "I walked a block up 16th and turned left at the newly opened Dave Cook Sporting Goods store on Larimer's…"

Dave Cook Sporting Goods (on the far right)

Denver Public Library, Western Collection Image File: ZZR710023472

"…and went into the building next to it. This was The Citizen's Mission, run by a Protestant church organization and strongly backed by a good city assemblyman… The Mission gave breakfast and supper to about two hundred men a day and in return had a well-attended bi-weekly church service…"

The Citizen Mission at 16<sup>th</sup> and Larimer (the sign is toward the bottom middle of the picture). It is between Surplus Sales and the Nugget Tap Room.

T.J. Noel Collection. Image File: ZZR710022661

"I went past some of Larimer's row of bars and pawn shops, then up 17<sup>th</sup> Street to the newly-created Federal Reserve Bank with its massive marble square-yard building blocks and with elegant iron bars protecting its windows... " NOTE: The old Federal Reserve Building was torn down and replaced by a structure at 1020 16<sup>th</sup> Street.

"Another left turn and along a block of Arapahoe Street whorehouses I later patroned."

NOTE: Denver shut down blatant houses of prostitution in 1915, including the House of Mirrors at 1942 Market. According to the plaque on the wall at 1942 Market, the House of Mirrors was "the classiest bordello in the Rocky Mountain West."

"Then right onto busy 18th Street with its noisy sheet metal shops and motorcycle showrooms and garages. Across Curtis Street's corner of candy company, parking lot, cheap hotel and cheaper restaurant, and up to Champa Street with the mighty colonnaded structure of the post office. Along this block I remember always hearing, from the depths of musty second-hand clothing stores, screech sounds of serious adolescent violin lessons."

The old Colorado Candy Company at 18th and Curtis

Denver Public Library. Western History Collection.

"On the Post Office corner I would pause for a quick drink at the public fountain which, unlike most of Denver's, was not shut off in the winter, so that conical ice attacked the spout's silvery knob, and on certain cold days it victoriously choked the bowl and froze the overflow basin outlet..."

The old downtown Denver Post Office (now the Byron White United States Courthouse) - 1823 Stout Street

Michael Reid 2015

The old Post Office is a thing of beauty. It sits on a pedestal surrounded by sidewalks, all made of Colorado marble. There are 16 columns at the front of the building. To get a sense of the scale of this place, you have to walk among these pillars. Look up and you'll see all the ledges are protected from the pigeons with netting (pigeon droppings discolor the marble).

"I'd next canter over to a huge stone bench whose giant size made even adults use only its edge for sitting. I made paradox of the puzzling proverb carved in its granite, for it cautioned against too much rest while offering it freely: 'Desire rest but desire not too much.'" NOTE: The exact quote on the bench is "If Thou Desire Rest Desire Not Too Much."

Michael Reid 2015

They really were on a "work and rest" theme when they built the old Post Office. The bench on the opposite side of the building says, "Alternate Rest And Labor Long Endure." (picture next page) It is unclear what this has to do with delivering the mail.

Michael Reid 2015

"A springing leap up the 18<sup>th</sup> Street side of broad stairway that circumvented the Post Office, to walk through the warmth of its block-long lobby... though on balmier days I disdained the minute of heat, and instead, scampered in a weaving run about the fluted sides of every enormous column that fronted Stout Street, a hundred feet of sidewalk-filled waste space between curb and building."

"Down the 19<sup>th</sup> Street steps three in a bound and catty-corner to a narrow wall's sharp peak which challenged the equilibrium. My tightrope was the angled top of a half-foot-high sidewalk border enclosing the grounds of the new Federal Building..."

This is the "new Federal Building" Cassady talks about. It is called The Federal Building and U.S. Custom House and was completed in 1931 when Cassady was five years old. It is located at 721 19th Street.

Michael Reid 2015

"Across California Street to go into the alley behind the basement Church of the Holy Ghost (where I once served a year as altar boy without missing a day), then under a vacant lot's billboard to reach the five-pointed intersection of Welton, Broadway and 20th Avenue."

Church of The Holy Ghost, dwarfed by the glass office tower behind it.   The church serves hot meals to the homeless six days a week.   It is located at 1900 California St.

Michael Reid 2015

"For the block I would walk it, 20th Avenue had one-way automobile traffic because it was so narrow.   On one side of its much-traveled ribbon of pavement, which terminated here, the triangular Crest Hotel rose in ten luxurious floors." (See the picture of the Crest below.   It had 6 floors, not 10.)

Denver Public Library. Western History Collection.

"From the beginnings of its swell near Welton Street to its upper end on Sherman, the hill of this 20th Avenue street surface was fully two blocks long and on my path from Lincoln to Glenarm was easily a hundred yards in width. "

"Reaching the sidewalk of Glenarm Street with my lungs in double tempo, I would pass a business school (later part of the University of Denver) and beyond that corner the first of the homes that fringed the downtown area. They nestled between a splendid Catholic Church, with matching slender spires of rough stone and the Denver Bible Institute whose odd belfry was a squat clapboard affair..."

NOTE: Curtis Park is the Denver neighborhood where Cassady lived and went to elementary school. It is close to Five Points, where Cassady and Kerouac went for jazz.

NOTE: The church mentioned above is not a Catholic church, but St. Andrews Episcopal Church at 2015 Glenarm Place. It was built in 1908.

Michael Reid 2015

"Now the residential section began in earnest and, from 21$^{st}$ Street to 22$^{nd}$, only a tiny candy store disturbed the rows of solidly bunched houses."

The house below is an example of the beautifully restored homes on Glenarm between 21$^{st}$ and 22$^{nd}$. Cassady passed this house every day on his way to and from school.

Michael Reid 2015

"I cut the corner and entered the far side of Ebert's huge gravel playground and ran its length in full tilt, even though the final spurt was not always enough to beat the school bell, for the bell was usually ringing."

**Walking Tour - Neal Cassady's route from The Metropolitan Hotel to Ebert Elementary**

If you're up to it, walk the route. It is 14 blocks one way. Six-year-old Neal walked the 14 blocks every day to Ebert and then back home to the Metropolitan.

1. Start at where the **Metropolitan Hotel** used to be - Market and 16$^{th}$ Street Mall.

2. Walk toward **Larimer Street** (1 block).

3. Turn **LEFT at Larimer** (Dave Cook's and the Citizen Mission used to be on this block) - (go 1 block to 17$^{th}$ Street).

4. **RIGHT onto 17$^{th}$ Street** (go 2 blocks to Arapahoe).

5. **LEFT on Arapahoe** (go 1 block to 18$^{th}$ Street).

6. **RIGHT on 18$^{th}$ Street** (go three blocks to Stout).

7. **LEFT onto Stout Street** (you're at the old Post Office; now Byron White Courthouse) - (go a block to 19$^{th}$ Street).

8. **RIGHT on 19$^{th}$ Street** (you're at the Federal Building and Customs House; Holy Ghost Church is at 19$^{th}$ and California).

9. **Cross Broadway and go to 20$^{th}$ Avenue** (continue on 20$^{th}$ Avenue to Glenarm).

10. **LEFT on Glenarm Place** (go 3 blocks to Ebert Elementary) (St. Andrews episcopal Church is on Glenarm as well as the houses Cassady passed every day on the way to and from school).

## Abandoned at 22<sup>nd</sup> and Larimer

Cody's father [Neal Cassady's father] and another alcoholic "got together a handful of greasy quarters, bought wire, screen, cloth and sewing needles and made hundreds of flyswatters... they headed for Nebraska to sell door to door [with little Cody in the back seat of the car]... They sold their pathetic flyswatters at the backdoors of farms... They returned clonking up Larimer with about eighteen dollars [and went on] a vast drunk that lasted five days... [leaving the car parked at Larimer and 22<sup>nd</sup> with Cody asleep in the backseat]... So when Cody woke up in the car on a cold clear October morning and didn't know what to do, Gaga, the beggar without legs who clattered tragically on his rollerboard on Wazee Street, took him in, fed him and made him a bed on the floor like a bed of straw and spent the night thundering around in bulge-eyed sweat trying to catch him in a foul hairy embrace that would have succeeded if he'd had legs or Cody hadn't lowered himself out of the transom." *Visions of Cody*, Jack Kerouac. Kindle Edition, 1993.

22<sup>nd</sup> Street and Larimer – Little Neal was left in the car

Michael Reid 2015

68

## Other hotels

Growing up with his alcoholic father, Neal Cassady was on intimate terms with the down-and-out hotels of downtown Denver.

"... Hotel Victor, overshadowed on its 18th and Larimer corner by Hotel Windsor, whose warm lobby we often used for 500 Rummy, played to 1 or 2,000 every sitting; Hotel Henry up Lawrence from 20th, an absolute morgue that later always came to mind whenever quiet buildings did; The Great Northern, a standard two-bit type on Larimer near 15th opposite the Crescent Moon, where I later sneak-shared one of Dad's women on a purely physical basis."
*The First Third*, Neal Cassady.

Not mentioned above, but one of the places Cassady and his father stayed was the St. Elmo Hotel, still standing at 1433 17th Street (below).

## Cassady childhood home – 26<sup>th</sup> and Champa – and the Puritan Pie Company

In December, 1930, "Neal got a two-chair shop near the corner of 26$^{th}$ and Champa streets. In this sad little shop so filled with contention, Neal and Maude shared the last year of their pitiful marriage. Although food was short, at least there was always dessert, for in the middle of the next block was the Puritan Pie Company, and on many an illegal Sunday the shop shades were drawn as Neal cut an employee's hair in exchange for a pie or two." *The First Third & Other Writings*, Neal Cassady.

The sad little shop at 26$^{th}$ and Champa – the small building 2$^{nd}$from the left with the white billboards. It has a dirt floor. The City of Denver has posted signs that the building will be demolished as a public nuisance and a danger to safety.

Photo: CPR/Hart Van Denburg

70

The Puritan Pie Company – just down the street from the "sad little shop."

Michael Reid 2015

At one point the Puritan Pie Company also made coconut honey macaroons. The Puritan Pie Company building has been unoccupied for decades.

## Cassady childhood home -- The Snowden Apartments
### The Snowden - 2563 Champa Street/910 26th Street

"There had been an agreement reached: henceforth I was to stay with Father only the 90 days of summer and with Mother during the school year... in a building on the corner of 26th and Champa Streets... called The Snowden... "
*The First Third & Other Writings*, Neal Cassady.

"... although the Snowden occupants were all poor, or perhaps more so because of it, they rocked the joint night and day, for the place had a noise mania; the air seemed always filled with assorted yelping catcalls, shouted curses, frightened screams and, topping all in my mind, those exciting feminine whoops of laughter.  There was hardly a moment when something untoward wasn't happening..."
*The First Third & Other Writings*, Neal Cassady.

Townhouses on the site of the former Snowden Apartments

Michael Reid 2015

72

**Neal's route from the Snowden Apartments to Ebert Elementary** (as described in *The First Third* by Neal Cassady)

1. **Start at 26$^{6th}$ Street and Champa. Take Champa to 25$^{th}$ Street.**
   "From 26$^{th}$ Street down the previously described block of Champa, turn at the line of shoddy tenements."

2. **Turn LEFT on 25$^{th}$ Street.**
   "On my left a vacant lot offset behind The Avery, and up 25$^{th}$ Street one block to The Style Inn on Stout's corner." [Note: The Avery is still there. It was built in 1904.]

3. **Turn RIGHT on Stout Street.**
   "Then down Stout Street past rows of apartment houses to 24$^{th}$'s corner of grocery, private homes and another beer joint."

4. **Turn LEFT on 24$^{th}$ Street.**
   "Up 24$^{th}$ a block to California's corner of vacant lot, large and modern domed auditorium of Negro church, lawn before huge natural gas tank that filled a half-block, and the ballpark [Sonny Lawson Field]."

   NOTE: The church is the Central Baptist Church at 670 24$^{th}$ Street, right across from Sonny Lawson Park. It was built in the late 1800's, although there have been a number of additions since.

5. **RIGHT onto California.** NOTE: Cassady cut across Sonny Lawson Field to get to Ebert. You cannot do that now. The field is fenced and locked to keep the homeless from camping on the grass.

"Bisecting this unfenced square block of dirt where I was to spend all my free time for many years [again, Sonny Lawson Field], to gain 23$^{rd}$ and Welton's corner of ballground, N.Y. Furniture Co.  (on alley behind which was an old man's shoeshop next to the first of Dad's barber shops) and its catty-corner stove and refrigerator warehouse, and lastly, a vacant building in the double-big first storied and wood-windowed elongated Parisian-like atticked row of shops-once-houses up which I went to cross the alley beyond and past the principal shop (to us kids anyhow), a candy store that was owned by stinking woman with a hundred cats... "

6.  **GO TO Park Avenue West.  LEFT on Park Avenue West.** Ebert is up two blocks – 410 Park Avenue West

## Cassady childhood home at 32$^{nd}$ and Marion

From the Snowden, Neal, his mother and other family members moved in across the alley from a friend's duplex at 32$^{nd}$ and Downing. "While this house, a sturdy two-storey affair facing Marion Street, was not long our home... it is well remembered for a lot happened there." By "a lot," Cassady means a sexual encounter with a young girl that was interrupted by her parents.

The house below is where "a lot happened." – 3135 Marion. The duplex across the alley consists of a couple of tiny wooden shacks.

Michael Reid 2015

## Barnum neighborhood of Denver

Neal and his father moved into a barn with one of Neal Sr.'s drinking buddies, his wife and twelve children. The barn was in the Barnum neighborhood of Denver. In *The First Third*, Cassady talks about the oldest sons having sex with their sisters. "I soon followed the leader in screwing all the sisters small enough to hold down- and those bold enough to lead."

The Barnum neighborhood is still in Denver. The neighborhood's boundaries are Sixth Avenue, Federal Boulevard, Alameda Avenue and Perry Street. About 6,500 people live in Barnum.

Here is what *Westword* has to say about the Barnum neighborhood. "Conceived for the working class, it continues to cater to exactly that set, and it shows. Get rid of the cockroaches in your house and more will just move in; during the summer, they hang out on the corner like they're selling drugs. The alleys smell like trash to the point that they're nauseating to walk down, but take care when you're walking down the street, because when you live in a poor neighborhood, you apparently don't consistently need sidewalks …"*O, Barnum! An ode to Denver's least desirable neighborhood*, by Jeff Otte in *Westword* Nov 10, 2011.

"Front porch chillin': A favorite occupation of what I like to call 'the Barnumployed.'" Jeff Ott in *Westword*, November 10, 2011.

## Cassady childhood home - Kingston Row Townhouses
## 411 and 407 21st Street

As a child, Neal lived in two of the Kingston Row Townhouses – units 411 and 407. Built in 1896, these may have been fleabags when Cassady lived there, but they are gorgeous now. The last time 411 sold (3/13/2014), it went for $448,000 .

Michael Reid 2015

**Tour -- Five Points and Curtis Park**

NOTE: Curtis Park is the Denver neighborhood where Cassady lived as a child and went to elementary school. It is close to Five Points, where Cassady and Kerouac went for jazz.

1. **START at Five Points - 27<sup>th</sup> Street and Welton.**

2. **The Rossonian Hotel** is located on the corner.

3. **Cervantes Masterpiece Ballroom** (formerly the Casino Cabaret) is across the street from the Rossonian - **2635 Welton St.**

4. **The Denver Kush Club** – a few doors down from Cervantes Masterpiece Ballroom - **2615 Welton.**

5. **The Roxy** is in the next block -- **2549 Welton St.**

6. **GO TO 26<sup>th</sup> and Champa. The "sad little shop."**
   - From the Rossonian Hotel, go east on Welton to 27<sup>th</sup> Street (just a few feet).
   - **LEFT on 27<sup>th</sup> Street** (go 1 block to California).
   - **RIGHT onto California** (go 1 block to 26<sup>th</sup> Street).
   - **RIGHT on 26<sup>th</sup> Street** (go 2 blocks to Champa).
   - **LEFT on Champa.**

7. **Snowden Apartments.** The site of the former Snowden Apartments is right across the street from the "sad little shop." **2563 Champa Street.**

8. **The Puritan Pie Company.** The Puritan Pie Company is catty corner from the Snowden Apartments at 26<sup>th</sup> and Champa.

9. **GO TO Sonny Lawson Field - 2301 Welton Street.**
   - From 26<sup>th</sup> and Champa, take Champa 3 blocks toward downtown.
   - **LEFT on Park Avenue W** (go 2 blocks to California).
   - Sonny Lawson Field is on the left between California and Welton.

**10. GO TO Ebert Elementary - 410 Park Ave W.**
- From Park Avenue W. and Welton, go to 410 Park Avenue West (1 block away)

**11. GO TO THE Kingston Row Townhouses - 411 and 407 21$^{st}$ Street.**
- From 410 Park Avenue W, go to Tremont.
- **RIGHT on Tremont** (go to 21$^{st}$ Street).
- **RIGHT on 21$^{st}$ Street.** The destination is on your right. - 411 and 407 21$^{st}$ Street.

## J.K. Mullen Home For Boys
## 3601 South Lowell Boulevard

www.mullenhigh.com/

Due to his chaotic family situation, Neal was sent to the J.K. Mullen Home For Boys in a suburb of Denver. He lived there for six months and then stole some athletic equipment and ran away.

In Cassady's time, Mullen was a school for orphan boys who went to classes and worked on the school's dairy farm. J.K. Mullen Home for Boys eventually became Mullen High School, a Catholic institution within the Archdiocese of Denver.

History of Mullen

1931-1950. School for orphan boys only. They went to school and worked in the dairy farm.

1950-1965. Accepted paying boarders and day students in addition to orphans. The dairy farm was discontinued and the name was changed to J.K. Mullen High School.

1966-1989. The last of the orphans graduated and boarding was terminated. The school became a four-year college preparatory high school for boys only.

1989-present. Mullen is a co-educational high school.

## Cassady stayed here - 2259 Gilpin

"Neal was now almost constantly on the move, staying with friends until his welcome wore out. So it was in October 1941, that he found himself sitting naked and eating breakfast, in the kitchen of a house in the 2200 block of Gilpin Street, the home of John and Lucille Walters, an amiable couple of elderly alcoholics who allowed all types of waifs and strays to share their home." [Neal met his friend Justin Brierly while eating breakfast naked at this house. Brierly was the Walters' nephew.] *Neal Cassady: The Fast Life of a Beat* Hero by Graham Vickers.

In the kitchen in this house, a naked Neal Cassady ate his breakfast.

Michael Reid 2015

81

## Colorado State Reformatory
## Buena Vista, Colorado

In 1944, Cassady spent 11 months at the Colorado State Reformatory in Buena Vista for receiving stolen property. Buena Vista is in the mountains about 2 ½ hours from Denver.

Old postcard of the Colorado State Reformatory in Buena Vista

The Colorado State Reformatory, Buena Vista, Chaffee County, Colo.

www.epodunk.com

While in the Reformatory, Cassady wrote letters to his friend Justin Brierly. Here are some excerpts.

Letter from Neal Cassady to Justin Brierly. October 8, 1944 "Here is a typical day:  Get up at 4 A.M., milk 8 cows till 6:45.  Take the cows to pasture, eat at 6:45, clean car barn from 7:15 to 9:30, then miscellaneous duties until noon, eat, grind corn or haul hay until 2:30, take a nap until 3:30, go get cows, eat at 5 P.M., milk cows again from 6:00 to 8:30, carry milk to kitchen, go to bed at 9:30 P.M."
*Neal Cassady Collected Letters, 1944 - 1967.*  Edited by Dave Moore.

Letter from Neal Cassady to Justin Brierly. October 23, 1944

"Please excuse the penmanship, as I can only see out of one eye; this morning I took the cows out to pasture, but on the way they ran out of the road into the corn field. The jackass I was riding couldn't run fast enough, so I jumped off & started to tie him to a barbed wire fence so I could chase the cows on foot. Just as I had tied the reins to the wire he jerked so hard it pulled a staple out of the fence post and into my left eye. It gorged a chunk out of my eyeball, but luckily failed to hit the cornea. I may lose the eye."
*Neal Cassady Collected Letters, 1944 - 1967.*

Letter from Neal Cassady to Justin Brierly. January 8, 1945
"Since I have last written you I have lost my job in the dairy barn (for hitting a cow) & since Dec.10 have been shoveling sheep manure for my keep..."
*Neal Cassady Collected Letters, 1944 - 1967.*

## Cassady apartment - 1073 Downing

Cassady had a basement apartment here in 1947 (he was 21 years old). He wrote letters to Ginsberg and Kerouac from this address.

1073 Downing – The house is still split up into apartments. There are five mailboxes on the front porch.

Michael Reid 2015

**Cassady address - 1242 Clarkson**

Cassady wrote letters from this address in 1947 and used it as a mail drop when he left town. In a letter to Ginsberg in May 1947, he wrote, "You can write me at 1242 Clarkson and they'll forward it to me." *Neal Cassady's Collected Letters, 1944 - 1967.* Edited by Dave Moore.

1242 Clarkson

Michael Reid 2015

## Send my pants -- 1156 Gaylord Denver

In March 1947, Cassady asks Ginsberg to send him a pair of pants he left behind in New York.
"... you must send the trousers in this fashion:

Bill Barnett
1156 Gaylord
Denver, Colorado"

*Neal Cassady Collected Letters, 1947 - 1967.* Edited by Dave Moore.

1156 Gaylord is the unit on the left of this duplex.

Michael Reid 2015

## Colburn Hotel and Apartments
## 980 Grant Street

Carolyn and Neal Cassady first met at the Colburn. She lived in apartment 306.

Here is what Carolyn says about their first meeting. "I could only stare, flustered by seeing the myth made flesh. Neal nodded, and in that instant the sweep of his blue eyes made me feel I had been thoroughly appraised... [He had a] Runyonesque flavor, a dangerous glamor heightened by the white T-shirt and bare muscular arms." *Off the Road: My Years with Cassady, Kerouac and Ginsberg*, Carolyn Cassady.

The Colburn Hotel opened in 1928 and was so popular, the owners decided to build a second tower. The Colburn Apartments opened in 1930. Originally upscale apartments, the building now rents to people of more modest means. The picture below is of the Colburn Hotel. The apartment tower is just to the south of the hotel.

Michael Reid 2015

## Midget Auto Races

Midget race cars - Denver 1947

autoracingmemories.com

In *On the Road*, Carlo Marx (Allen Ginsberg) is telling Sal Paradise (Jack Kerouac), "Dean [Neal Cassady] and I are embarked on a tremendous season together. We are trying to communicate with absolute honesty and absolute completeness everything on our minds. We've had to take Benzedrine. We sit on the bed cross-legged, facing each other.... But he keeps rushing out to see the midget auto races." *On The Road*, Jack Kerouac.

Midget auto races were all the rage in Denver in 1947. There were two racetracks where Neal Cassady could have seen the races - Lakeside Speedway at the Lakeside Amusement Park and Englewood Speedway in a suburb just south of Denver. In 1947, Englewood Speedway was just an oval, dirt track without a grandstand. People sat on the grass to watch races. An industrial park currently sits on the former site of Englewood Speedway.

Lakeside Amusement Park operated Lakeside Speedway on the park grounds starting in the late 1930's. The track was a 1/5-mile oval. It is still there, but has not been used since 1988.

The track at Lakeside Speedway

The grandstand at Lakeside Speedway

## 1254 Fairfax and the Marion Inn

The following is from *Visions of Cody*.  Jack Kerouac and Neal Cassady are talking (Neal is "Cody" in the text below).

"Jack.  Earl Johnson?  Where is he?
Cody.  He's in Denver.... Earl is working for his father there, see that, ah, distributor for Old Forester whiskies or something, lots of money, see?
Jack.  In Denver?
Cody.  Yah and so Earl – Oh he's been there for years, yes-stepfather has loads of money, they live in that ritzy joint out there, Twelve fifty-four Fairfax... Fairfax Manor.
Jack.  Where Minko and I stayed in Ed Gray's pad, for the summer.
Cody.  Yeh that was across the street sort of but down the road awhile..."
"Cody.  ... we'd go to the bar, directly across the street, fifty yards from his house, we would sit there and drink beer – *you* know that little bar, the Marion Inn ... the little bar up there at Park, Seventeenth and Marion, Park Avenue also, it's a three-way intersection... I got so drunk in there that... Val would have to go home and I'd lay in the grass, beside the bar there, and I couldn't get up or anything..."
*Visions of Cody*, Jack Kerouac.

The three-way intersection at Park, 17th Avenue and Marion is still there, but no Marion Inn.  There is still a patch of grass in a small park at Marion and 17th.

Neal Cassady may have his streets mixed up.  No 1254 Fairfax address exists and the homes on that block are modest, middle-class dwellings.  There are no manors in sight.  When Kerouac says, "Where Minko and I stayed in Ed Gray's... pad for the summer," he is talking about the apartment at 1475 Cherry (Roland Major's apartment).  Cherry Street is five blocks east of Fairfax.

Places that are no more or never were

### Cassady's first childhood home in Denver - 23$^{rd}$ and Welton

Cassidy's family arrives in Denver in 1926. "There on 23$^{rd}$ Street between Welton and Glenarm next to the alleyway, was a brown brick building of miniature dimensions. It housed an incredibly cluttered shoe-repair shop, the accumulation of a half-century's leather litter. The old repairman who squatted daily before the ceiling-high barrier of sweepings that choked his shop, was Neal's [Neal Senior's] new landlord. His two-chair barber shop that shared the building with the shoe stall was acquired on a one-year's lease. Neal, Maude, Jimmy, Betty and little Neal moved into the crowded quarters in the rear of the shop." *The First Third & Other Writings*, Neal Cassady.

23$^{rrd}$ and Welton is now a vacant lot. It sits directly across the street from where Kerouac saw the softball game in the summer of 1949. It is also right around the corner from Ebert Elementary.

### Cassady childhood home - 22$^{nd}$ and Stout

"Neal's non-sobriety persisted as did the dwindling of customers, so that they just couldn't make ends meet, and Neal lost the shop, the last of several, early in 1932. He also lost his wife, who moved into an apartment at 22$^{nd}$ and Stout Streets... Little Neal went with his wino father into the lowest slums of Denver." *The First Third & Other Writings*, Neal Cassady.

The old buildings at 22$^{nd}$ and Stout have been torn down, replaced with a parking lot, apartments and businesses.

**Cassady childhood home - 20th St and Court Place**
The Great Crash of 1929 occurred. Everyone was broke. In 1930, the family moved into "an apartment above a noisy creamery at 20th and Court Place." *The First Third & Other Writings*, Neal Cassady.

There is no 20th Street and Court Place. Court Place ends at 17th Street, three blocks before 20th and picks up again at 22nd Street.

**Cassady crashed with friends here - 1830 Grant Street**
Cassady's friends, Helen and Ruth Gullion (the Bettencourt sisters in *On the Road*) lived here. Cassady stayed there from time to time. Allen Ginsberg also stayed there in the summer of 1947.

1830 now houses a modern office building. Just north of 1830, however, is an old down-and-out apartment building that looks like just the kind of place the Beats would have called home (corner of 19th Avenue and Grant Street). It is worth a trip to 19th and Grant to see this weathered, Spanish style building.

**Carlo Marx's apartment**
**9th Avenue and Grant Street**
Carlo Marx in *On the Road* is based on Allen Ginsberg. "Carlo's basement apartment was on Grant Street in an old red-brick rooming house near a church. You went down an alley, down some stone steps, opened an old raw door, and went through a kind of cellar till you came to his board door."

The apartment was at 9th Avenue and Grant. The apartment building was torn down and The Denver Public Schools Administrative Building is at that site now.

Neal Cassady's formal education was in the Denver Public Schools. He attended Ebert Elementary (starting Ebert at age 5), Cole Junior High - age 11 and East High - age 15. Cassady attended East intermittently and did not graduate.

**Ebert Elementary**
**410 Park Avenue West**
"The first convenient Monday after we settled into the Metropolitan, Dad put me back in school... Onto the big yellow streetcar for a quick ride up Sixteenth to Welton, then left to an alignment on 23$^{rd}$ Street. On the block-long walk to our Glenarm Street destination, we paused a moment to stare as Dad pointed out all the cluttered maze behind the window of the shoe cobbler's next to his first Denver barber shop. Then we entered the modern building of gleaming white firebrick that is Ebert Grammar School... I went to Ebert six straight years." *The First Third & Other Writings*, Neal Cassady.

Ebert is now a school for gifted and talented children. Its formal name is Polaris at Ebert Elementary. Kerouac's baseball field at 23$^{rd}$ and Welton is just down the street.

Ebert Elementary

www.10best.com

93

## Cole Junior High
## 3240 Humboldt Street

Cassady developed a pattern of truancy at Cole, something that intensified when he went on to East High.

Cole Junior High has fallen on hard times since Cassady's day. It draws mostly from poor neighborhoods and was closed by the state in 2005 due to consistently poor scores on state tests. Cole is now a charter school and part of the Denver School of Science and Technology Program.

In 2004, Governor John Hickenlooper made the "Cole Pledge" - every student at Cole on the day the pledge was made would have money to go to college. A little more than 10% of those students have taken advantage of the pledge (58% of students system-wide in the Denver Public Schools enroll in college or some other form of post-secondary education).

Cole Junior High School

City Data Forum

94

## East High School
### 1600 City Park Esplanade

Neal Cassady started at East High School, but did not attend regularly. He never came close to graduating.

Opening in 1874, East was the first high school in Denver and it is recognized as one of America's top high schools. Douglas Fairbanks, one of the great silent movie stars, was expelled from East. Other famous graduates include Judy Collins, Don Cheadle, Mamie Eisenhower, Pam Grier, Sidney Sheldon (the man who created *I Dream of Jeannie*), astronaut Jack Swigert and Hattie McDaniel, the first African American to win an Academy Award (for her performance in *Gone with the Wind*).

East High School

City Data Forum

## Cassady's Saturday routine as a child

"Today on the lower side of Larimer between 17<sup>th</sup> and 18<sup>th</sup>, there is only one 'Zaza.' In my time there were two, but the theater which once shared the name has since become the 'Kiva.' The barbershop Zaza, next to the theater [was owned by Charlie]... Charlie, from the lead chair, ran the shop with a quiet dignity uncommon to any Skid Row." *The First Third & Other Writings*, Neal Cassady. City Lights, 1971.

"Each Saturday's routine was similar; we left the Metropolitan, ate breakfast and went to Charley's three-chair shop together, and while Dad worked on his infrequent morning customers or sat in the battered barber chair to rest his feet, I absorbed what I could of *Liberty Magazine* and the *Rocky Mountain News*... I waited for the Zaza next door to open... Now this showcase was absolutely Denver's worst and catered to correspondingly poor clientele. Paying ten cents admission, anyone (except children who were admitted for a nickel) could sit in the filth of its interior to watch Hollywood magic for more than half the day before seeing the same scene twice." *The First Third & Other Writings*, Neal Cassady.

Writing about the odor in the Zaza Theater, Neal said: "Naturally, I can call up only a fraction of this Great Smell's many component parts and cannot fully imagine whence its source, but... each patron's shared odor added to the building's own array to form a complicated multiplicity of rot while permeating the nostrils with such a potency that, while struggling to accustom, I breathed as little air as possible through my open mouth." *The First Third & Other Writings*, Neal Cassady.

Neither the Zaza barshop nor the Zaza Theater exist today.

**Neal Cassady's Sunday routine as a child** (as described in *The First Third & Other Writings*, Neal Cassady.)

On Sundays, Neal's father "managed to struggle awake in time for our late breakfast at the Mission. Leisurely, we doubled back toward 16$^{th}$ and went down its Sabbath-deserted street in an erratic walk.. Again passing the Metropolitan, we would usually pause in our trek to chat with the old boys who, ungracefully decorating the front steps with their unsavory selves, crowded weakly around the spit-spattered doorway so as to soak up what strength they could by a moment in the sun... "

"From Market to Wynkoop Streets were four short blocks... the Union Station at the foot of 17$^{th}$ Street came into view, and unless Dad's firmly-believed-in restroom call made detour necessary, we avoided the building because of the deadend tarnished tracks on its other side."

Union Station

"Instead, angling left, circling busy men loading mail and baggage in the cars just behind the hissing engines, we took to 15<sup>th</sup> Street's chuck-holed pavement to cross the tracks. "

"Where the South Platte River passes beneath the 15<sup>th</sup> Street bridge of angle-iron and wood that sqeaked along in protests as autos passed over its rapidly deteriorating surface, we would climb down a dozen or so feet to the gravel bed where most of our Sunday PM's were spent, strolling to and fro over the several hundred yards of semi-beach between 15<sup>th</sup> and 17<sup>th</sup> Streets. Here my strongest concern was skipping rocks over the water...

The South Platte looking toward the "semi-beach" between 15<sup>th</sup> and 17<sup>th</sup> streets. Neal played here Sundays as a child.

Michael Reid 2015

## Cherry Creek from downtown to University

"In the next few years of pre-adolescence, all the city was to become my playground... so that even the many trickle-dry miles of Cherry Creek, hardly trudged upon since prospector days (from its union with the Platte at 14th through all busy downtown and residential district alongside Speer Blvd... to University Avenue and onward, without roadway, to its upper reaches well past Denver's southeastern limits.."
*The First Third*, Neal Cassady.

Now there is a bike path all the way from downtown to University and beyond.

www.9news.com

## Confluence of Cherry Creek and the South Platte River

"... in the earlier years on these always exciting excursions of exploration, I lingered most and learned to swim a little... under 14th's viaduct where the junction of Cherry Creek and the here-sewered Platte had been damned up over my head's height, so that Intercity electrical plant could have power." *The First Third*, Neal Cassady.

The confluence of Cherry Creek (to the far left) and the South Platte River

Michael Reid 2015

Just across the river from where this picture was taken is the old Denver Tramway Building (located at 1416 Platte Street), now the Denver headquarters for REI. Cassady would have seen the DTC building every time he visited the Cherry Creek/South Platte confluence.

## Pederson's Pool Hall
## 1523 Glenarm

Just out of the State Reformatory in 1945, Cassady began spending his time Pederson's Pool Hall.

Here is what Cassady wrote Jack Kerouac about Pederson's [letter to Kerouac December 17, 1950]: "Off to the poolhall, back to the old grind; I seemed to have a mania. From the way I loafed there all day one would scarcely believe I'd never been seen in a poolhall two short years before..." *Neal Cassady Collected Letters, 1944 - 1967*

Pederson's is long gone, replaced by the Denver Pavilions complex that includes stores such as Forever 21, Banana Republic and the Gap.

It is still worth a walk by. Cassady spent quite a bit of time lounging in Pederson's and you might pick up his vibe.

Denver Pavilions

www.gartproperties.com

## A bar on East Colfax Avenue

Letter from Cassady to Kerouac Dec 17, 1950. "The route from 12$^{th}$ and Ogden to 16$^{th}$ and Lincoln lies for the most part, if one so desires, along Colfax Avenue. Horrible mistake, stupid moment; I chose a path just to dig people on the crowded thoroughfare as I hustled by them. At midblock between Pennsylvania and Pearl Sts. is a tavern whose plateglass front ill-conceals the patrons of it booths. I was almost past this bar when I glanced up to see my younger blood-brother inside drinking beer alone. I had made good time and the hard habit of lushing that I was then addicted to pushed me through the door to bum a quickie off him." *Neal Cassady Collected Letters, 1944 - 1967.* Edited by Dave Moore.

Martha's Beauty Salon and Pete's Café and Steakhouse are right about where the bar Cassady mentions used to be. Pete's is a long-time Denver café. Great cheap hole in the wall diner." - Pete Johnson, Foursquare, 2014.

Michael Reid 2015

## Gates Rubber Company – 999 South Broadway

Neal Cassady was on the night shift at Gates Rubber Company by the age of 13. He worked recapping tires, a job he would do periodically throughout his travels. Gates was one of the biggest employers in Denver with a payroll of over 5,000. Manufacturing stopped in 1991 and the factory was torn down in 2014 to make way for new development. The Gates Corporation, however is still in business and is a world leader in the manufacture of power transmission belts.

The old Gates Rubber factory before it was demolished

"Gates Factory" by Plazak at en.wikipedia. Licensed under CC BY 3.0 via Wikimedia Commons

**Neal Cassady looking for his father**

Dean Moriarity (Neal Cassady) looking for his father: "This afternoon, man, I went down to Jiggs' Buffet where he used to pour draft beer in tender beffudlement and get hell from the boss and go staggering out- no- and I went to the old barbershop next to the Windsor- no, not there – old fella told me he thought he was – imagine! – working in a railway gandy-dancing cookshack or sumpin for the Boston and Maine in New England!" *On the Road*, Jack Kerouac.

Neal Cassady Sr. is on the left

## The old Denver Public Library building
## Civic Center Park - 15<sup>th</sup> and Broadway

Neal Cassady met Hal Chase at the old Denver Public Library. Chase was a student at Columbia University and Cassady later visited him in New York City, where he met Jack Kerouac and Allen Ginsberg. Chase introduced Cassady to swallowing the strips from Benzedrine inhalers. Cassady shared his girlfriend Mary Ann Freeland with Chase.

Denver Central Library, a Greek temple design, was funded by Andrew Carnegie and opened in 1910. The old library lasted for 45 years until a new Denver main library opened in 1956 at Broadway and 14$^{th}$. The old library is still in Civic Center Park, but called The McNichols Civic Center Building (in honor of a former mayor of Denver).

Michael Reid 2015

## "Jack Was Here" and The Oasis

"In 2011, an elite team of street thugs (guys you really don't want to mess with - so don't go squealing to the coppers) set out to pay tribute to Jack Kerouac's various visits to Denver, CO. Armed with a stencil, a couple cans of spray paint, and a list of locations, these thugs tagged and photographed the iconic writer's known haunts around the city."
jack-was-here.tumblr.com/

NOTE: Many of the stencils have been covered over or removed. Below is a picture of a "street thug" stenciling a Kerouac likeness on a wall close to the former Oasis.

"The Oasis was located at 1729 E. Colfax Ave. where a Taco Bell now stands. The old establishment used to serve milkshakes and cheeseburgers to East High students and the like and was frequented by Neal Cassady. He used to ditch his afternoon classes to steal a car, pick a girl up at The Oasis, and then drive her to the mountains for the night. Kerouac, a fan of good looking Denver girls, visited The Oasis a couple of times while he was in Denver." jack-was-here.tumblr.com/

## Mount Olivet Cemetery
## 12801 W. 44th Ave, Wheat Ridge, CO 80033

Neal Cassady's parents – Neal Sr. and Maud - are buried in Mount Olivet Cemetery in Wheat Ridge. Mount Olivet is a Roman Catholic Cemetery founded in 1892 by the Archdiocese of Denver.

"Neal's site is Section 26, Block 5, Lot 6, Grave 9. Once at the correct Section and Block, looking east, count back nine rows and then step north three paces (assuming you are on the south side of the Block.) Neal's site is one grave south of Maria C. Lopez. High tech GPS version: N 39.78387, W105.14188. That will put you within a 15' circle of error." NOTE: Neal's grave is unmarked (at the time of his death, he was indigent and the Catholic Church undertook the cost of his burial). www.pbase.com/pzo/ncgravesite

Neal is in Section 26, Block 5, Lot 6, Space 9 in an unmarked grave. He is in the same lot as the Bebo family. www.findagrave.com/php

**Mercury Cafe**
**2199 California Street**

The Mercury Café was not open when the Beats were in Denver, but it throws a Neal Cassady birthday bash in February each year. It is a fun time for Cassady fans.

Mercury Café

**"Neal Cassady:  The Denver Years."**

CPT12

"Neal Cassady: The Denver Years" is a documentary produced by Colorado Public Television, Channel 12.

The film has interviews with a number of beat figures including Carolyn Cassady, Lawrence Ferlinghetti, Ed White and Al Hinkle.

# Allen Ginsberg
# Denver and Boulder

## Allen Ginsberg talks about Denver

WARNING: Some of the excerpts from Ginsberg works are sexually graphic.

"17 May, 1972. Drove all afternoon with Bob Burford thru Denver, saw Ed White's Botanical Plastic Concrete Gazebo hothouse- Justin Brierly's old family house now tattered, Hal Chase's demolished homesite, the Grant Street Block where I lived & fucked Neal in the mouth ('I feel like an old whore.'), Sherman Street where the Gillion sisters, nurses lovers of Jack, Neal, Bob, Ed? Live in apartment on whose floor I slept, the Apartment back porch where Ed White and Alan Temko lived, East High where Justin took Neal, the Capital Lawn where Bob and I this day wrote Peace Vigil appeal to Gov. Love..."
*The Visions of the Great Remember*, Allen Ginsberg. Included in the Kindle edition of *Visions of Cody*.

### Howl

"...who journeyed to Denver, who died in Denver, who came back to Denver & waited in vain, who watched over Denver & brooded & loned in Denver and finally went away to find out the Time, & now Denver is lonesome for her heroes..." — Allen Ginsberg, *Howl and Other Poems*. City Lights. 1956.

"N.C., secret hero of these poems, cocksman and Adonis of Denver-joy to the memory of his innumerable lays of girls in empty lots & diner backyards, moviehouses' rickety rows, on mountaintops in caves or with gaunt waitresses in familiar lonely petticoat upliftings & especially secret gas-station solipsisms of johns, & hometown alleys too..." -- Allen Ginsberg, *Howl and Other Poems*. City Lights. 1956.

## Jack Kerouac School - located at Naropa University
## 2130 Arapahoe Ave, Boulder, CO 80302

Naropa University is a Buddhist-inspired, liberal arts college in Boulder, Colorado.

Allen Ginsberg and Anne Waldman founded the Jack Kerouac School at Naropa University. The school "emphasizes innovative approaches to literary arts. Our programs problematize genre while cultivating contemplative and experimental writing practices." Naropa website.

Sam Kashner was the only student at the Jack Kerouac School the first year it opened. He describes his experiences in *When I Was Cool. My Life at the Jack Kerouac School*. Here is what he writes about the original Naropa facilities. "To get to the Jack Kerouac School of Disembodied Poetics, you had to get to the mall on Pearl Street in downtown Boulder, and then climb the stairs next to the New York Delicatessen..." (The same delicatessen that was in the old sitcom *Mork and Mindy*.) Naropa offices were at 1111 Pearl Street.

Naropa University now (not the one on the mall)

en.wikipedia.org

**The New York Delicatessen - Pearl Street Mall, 1117 Pearl St, Boulder (closed)**

"We [Sam Kashner and Billy Burroughs, Jr - William Burroughs's son] walked over to Burroughs apartment and then to the New York Deli. On the way, I walked between father and son, who had nothing to say to each other." *When I Was Cool. My Life at the Jack Kerouac School.* Sam Kashner. Perennial. 2005.

**Mork And Mindy' Deli Closes, To Be Replaced By Sushi Bar.** June 17, 1999. *Chicago Tribune.*
"The deli whose exterior was featured in the 1970s TV series 'Mork and Mindy' has served its last corned beef on rye." A sushi bar will replace it. "'Mork doesn't work at the New York Deli anymore, and he hasn't for years,' Boulder Daily Camera food editor John Lehndorff said. 'Slowly, the independent restaurants are being replaced. We now have three sushi bars downtown, and I'm not sure what that means.'"

The exterior of the old New York Delicatessen, Boulder (now the home of the Haka Sushi Grill and Sake Bar)

hapasushi.com

The Allen Ginsberg Library at Naropa University
2130 Arapahoe Road in Boulder

www.naropa.edu

Michael Reid 2015

**Ginsberg and Burroughs lived here**
**Varsity Townhouses. 1555 Broadway. Boulder, Colorado.**

"The first summer of Naropa, all the poets, writers, and musicians lived in the Varsity Apartments, down the hill from the University of Colorado... a three-story, slightly down-at-heels apartment complex with outdoor walkways that made it look like a prison compound." *When I Was Cool. My Life at the Jack Kerouac School*, Sam Kashner.

hotpads.com

NOTE: When I visited the Varsity, I asked a half dozen residents if they were aware that Allen Ginsberg and William Burroughs had lived there. None of them were. In fact, none of them knew who Ginsberg and Burroughs were.

Tom's Tavern - 1047 Pearl Street.  Boulder.
(closed in 2007)

bethpartin.com

"A few of us - Allen [Ginsberg], Anne [Waldman], Burroughs, Gregory [Corso], and I - walked over to Tom's Tavern after the reading." *When I Was Cool. My Life at the Jack Kerouac School*, Sam Kashner.  Perennial, 2005.

For over forty years, Tom's Tavern was a Boulder institution.  Its burger was regularly voted the best in town.  Tom's closed in 2007.  As one Tom's customer said when it was closed, "RIP brother. When I get to heaven, I know you'll be there, with your... half chicken meal for 7 bucks.  A pox on the yuppie fusion wine bar shit hole that takes the place of Toms."  Stan O on Yelp, 2009.

**Ginsberg lived here - 1001 Mapleton. Boulder, Colorado.**

Ginsberg's friend David Padwa owned this beautiful house. The foothills are a five-minute walk away. It is 4,400 square feet and has an estimated market value of $2.4 million.

Michael Reid 2015

**Ginsberg and Peter Orlovsky lived here - 2141 Bluff Street. Boulder, Colorado.**

This house is 1,490 square feet and was built in 1925. 2141 Bluff St is in the Whittier neighborhood in Boulder.

Michael Reid 2015

## Rocky Flats

The Rocky Flats Plant, located 30 minutes from Boulder, manufactured triggers for nuclear bombs. The plant caused extensive environmental damage during its operation from 1952 to 1992. Radioactive contamination spread outside the plant to areas east and south, including parts of Denver. Weapons production at the plant was halted after an FBI/EPA raid in 1989. As a result of the raid, individuals at the Rockwell Corporation, the plant operators, pleaded guilty to criminal charges.

Years of protest preceded the shutdown of the plant. Allen Ginsberg was one of the protesters. He, along with teachers and students at the Naropa Institute and others, were arrested for sitting on railroad tracks leading to the facility.

All this happened during Parent's Weekend at Naropa. Parents arrived at the Institute only to be told that their children were in jail and needed bail money.

Blocking the trains – Ginsberg, Orlovsky and students.

www.boulderweekly.com

## Shambala Mountain Center - Red Feather Lakes, Colorado

Allen Ginsberg was cremated. One third of his ashes are in his family plot in New Jersey, one third at Jewel Heart, Gelek Rinpoche's Sangha and one third at the Shambala Mountain Center near Red Feather Lakes, Colorado. Peter Orlovsky and Billy Burroughs (William Burroughs' son) are also buried at the Mountain Center.

Allen Ginsberg marker at the Shambala Mountain Center. It reads... "Dharma Lion, Allen Ginsberg, June 3, 1926 – April 5, 1997. ~my life work Poesy, transmitting that spontaneous awareness to Mankind (from Who)"

shambhalatimes.org

The **Shambhala Mountain Center** was founded by Chogyam Trungpa. It is a retreat on six hundred acres two hours north of Boulder. The center offers Shambala Training.

# More Self-Guided Tours

## West Denver/Longmont/Boulder - A Driving Tour

This tour will take you half a day to a day, depending on how much time you spend at each spot.

1. **START AT** Colfax Elementary School.   **1526 Tennyson**
   - Take Colfax Avenue west to Tennyson (44 blocks west of Broadway).

2. **GO TO 6100 W Center Avenue** (Kerouac's house in 1949)
   - From 1526 Tennyson, go west towards the mountains on W Colfax (go .5 miles on Colfax).
   - Turn left onto S/Sheridan Blvd (go 2 miles on S Sheridan)
   - Turn right onto W Alameda Ave (go .5 miles on W Alameda).
   - Turn left onto S Harlan St (go .4 miles on Harlan St.).
   - Turn right onto W Center Ave - destination is on the left - 6100 W Center Ave.

3. **GO TO Lakeside Amusement Park and Lakeside Speedway. 4601 Sheridan Blvd (gate admission is only $3)**
   - FROM 6100 W Center Avenue (10 - 15 minutes travel time).
   - Head east on W Center Ave toward S Harlan St (40 feet).
   - Turn left onto S Harlan St  (.4 miles on S Harlan).
   - Turn right onto W Alameda Avenue (.5 miles on W Alameda).
   - Turn left on Sheridan Blvd (4.7 miles on S Sheridan).
   - Destination will be on the left - 4601 S Sheridan Boulevard.

4. **Mount Olivet Cemetery. 12801 W. 44th Avenue in Wheat Ridge, Colorado.** (Neal Sr. is buried here)
   * From 4601 Sheridan Boulevard (30 – 35 minutes travel time).
   * Head north on S Sheridan Blvd toward W 48th Avenue (.3 miles).
   * Turn left onto W 48th Avenue (.5 miles).
   * Take the ramp on the left to I-70 West.
   * Merge onto I-70 West (3.8 miles).
   * Take exit 286/CO-72/Ward Road.
   * Left onto 286/CO-72/Ward Road (.2 miles).
   * Turn right onto W 44th Avenue – Destination is at 12801 W 44th Avenue.

5. **From Mt. Olivet to Longmont (Kerouac gas station) – across from 1114 Neon Forest Circle.**
   * Go east on 44th Avenue (.6 miles).
   * Turn left onto the I-70 East ramp (.3 miles).
   * Merge onto I-70 (2.4 miles).
   * Take exit 269 A/Wadsworth/CO-121.
   * Turn left on N Wadsworth/CO-121 (9.9 miles).
   * Continue on US 287 N (17.3 miles).
   * Turn left on Pike Road.
   * Take an immediate left on Kristy Court.
   * Left on Tenacity Drive.
   * Right on Ionosphere Street.
   * The gas station is at the end of the block -- corner of Ionosphere Street and Neon Forest Circle.
   * The gas station sits across the street from a building at 1114 Neon Forest Circle.

6. **From Longmont to Boulder (Ginsberg sites)**
   * Retrace your route back to Pike Road and US 287 N (Main Street).
   * Take a left on Main Street.
   * Go to CO 119 (Ken Pratt Boulevard).
   * Take a left on CO 119 (Ken Pratt Boulevard).

7. **Sites in Boulder**
   - Take CO 119 to Boulder (11 miles) – **the 1$^{st}$ destination is 1001 Mapleton. (Ginsberg lived here)**
   - Take the CO-119/Diagonal Hwy ramp.
   - Turn right onto CO-119/Diagonal Hwy (.7 miles).
   - Continue straight onto Iris Ave (1.3 miles).
   - Turn left onto CO-7 E/Broadway (1.1 miles).
   - Turn right onto Mapleton Ave – the destination will be on your right.

   - **From 1001 Mapleton, go to 2141 Bluff Street. (Ginsberg lived here)**
     - Head east on Mapleton Ave toward Broadway (.7 miles).
     - Turn left onto 20th St (375 feet).
     - Turn right at the 1st cross street onto Bluff St – destination is on the left.

   - **From 2141 Bluff Street, go to 1117 Pearl Street. (the old New York Deli; the first Naropa offices were at 1111 Pearl)**
     - Head west on Bluff St toward 21st St  (.1 miles).
     - Turn left onto 20th St (.2 miles).
     - Turn right at the 3rd cross street onto Spruce St (.1 miles).
     - At the traffic circle, continue straight to stay on Spruce St (.5 miles).
     - Turn left onto 11th St – the destination is on the left.

- From 1117 Pearl Street, go to 1555 Broadway. (Ginsberg lived here)
  - Take 11$^{th}$ St to CO 119.
  - Left on CO 119.
  - Right on Broadway - destination is on the right.

- **From 1555 Broadway, go to 2130 Arapahoe. (The Ginsberg Library and Naropa University)**
  - Head southeast on Broadway toward Grandview Ave (.2 miles).
  - Turn left onto University Ave (.2 miles).
  - Continue onto 17th St (.3 miles).
  - Turn right onto Arapahoe Ave – the destination will be on the left.

### Downtown - A Walking Tour

This is a pretty good hike, so wear your walking shoes. NOTE: There is some overlap between this tour and the Cassady route from the Metropolitan to Ebert.

1. **START AT the old Denver Public Library 144 W Colfax Ave.** (it is now the McNichols Civic Center).
   - See if anyone inside can show you exactly where Neal Cassady met Hal Chase.

2. **GO TO the old site of Pederson's Pool Hall at 1523 Glenarm.** Pederson's is gone, replaced by shops and restaurants, but Neal Cassady spent so much time here, you might still feel the vibe.
   - From 144 West Colfax Avenue, head east on W Colfax Ave toward 15th St (400 feet).
   - Turn left onto 15th St (.2 miles).
   - Turn right onto Glenarm Place (100 feet) - 1523 Glenarm is the old address.

3. **GO TO the Denver Dry Goods building, 16th and California.**
   - On Glenarm Pl head toward 16th St (400 feet).
   - Turn left onto 16th St.
   - Go to California Street - destination is at 16th and California.

4. **GO TO the Daniels & Fischer Tower, 1601 Arapahoe.**
   - From 16th and California...
   - TAKE 16th Street toward Stout.
   - Go 4 blocks to Arapahoe - 1601 Arapahoe.

5. **GO TO 14th and Larimer** - Larimer Square gives you a feeling for the old buildings that used to be in downtown Denver.
   - From 1601 Arapahoe.
   - Take Arapahoe toward 15th Street.
   - Go two bocks to 14th Street.
   - Take a right at 14th Street.
   - Go two blocks to Larimer. Right on Larimer. Larimer Square is between 14th and 15th on Larimer.

6. **GO TO 1433 17$^{th}$ Street** - The St. Elmo Hotel, one of the hotels in which Cassady and his father stayed.
   - Take Larimer toward 15$^{th}$ Street.
   - Go 3 blocks to 17$^{th}$ Street.
   - Left on 17$^{th}$ Street.
   - Go 1 ½ blocks to 1433 17$^{th}$ Street.

7. **GO TO 22$^{nd}$ and Larimer** - the corner where Neal was left in the car by his father.
   - Go up 17$^{th}$ Street to Larimer.
   - Right at Larimer Street.
   - Go 5 blocks to 22$^{nd}$ Street.

8. **GO TO Old Post Office** - between 18$^{th}$ & 19$^{th}$ on Stout.
   - From 22$^{nd}$ and Larimer, take Larimer back to 20$^{th}$ Street.
   - Left on 20$^{th}$ Street.
   - Go 5 blocks to Stout.
   - Turn right on Stout.
   - Go 1 block to 19$^{th}$ & Stout.

9. **GO TO The Federal Building at 721 19$^{th}$ Street.**
   - The Federal Building is across the street from the old Post Office.
   - Cross 19$^{th}$.
   - Turn right on 19$^{th}$.
   - Go to California.
   - Left on California.

10. **GO TO The Holy Ghost Church - 1900 California.**
    - The Holy Ghost Church is right across the street on California.

11. **GO TO the old Greyhound Terminal building at 1730 Glenarm.**
    - Take 19<sup>th</sup> toward Broadway.
    - Right on Broadway.
    - Right on Glenarm Place.
    - Go to 1730 Glenarm Place.

12. **GO TO the YMCA.  25 E 16th Ave.**
    - Take Glenarm to 17<sup>th</sup> Street.
    - Left on 17<sup>th</sup> Street.
    - Right on Broadway.
    - Left on 16<sup>th</sup> Avenue – Destination is 25 E 16<sup>th</sup> Avenue.

## Driving Tour – Houses and apartments

1. **START at 1475 East Cherry Street.** (46 blocks east of Broadway) - Roland Majors apartment.

2. **GO TO 1156 Gaylord.** ("send my pants to this address")
   - Head south on Cherry St toward E 13th Ave (.2 miles).
   - Turn right onto E 13th Ave (1.4 miles).
   - Turn left onto Gaylord St.
   - Destination will be on the left (.2 miles) – 1156 Gaylord.

3. **GO TO 1073 Downing.** (Neal Cassady lived here in a basement apartment). Head south on Gaylord St toward E 11th Ave (400 feet).
   - Turn left onto E 11th Ave (350 feet).
   - Turn right onto York St (.3 miles).
   - Turn right onto E 8th Ave (.7 miles).
   - Turn right onto Downing St (go almost 3 blocks).
   - Destination will be on the left – 1073 Downing.

4. **GO TO 1242 Clarkson.** (Neal Cassady stayed here)
   - Head north on Downing St toward E 12th Ave (.1 miles).
   - Turn left onto E 12th Ave (.2 miles).
   - Turn right onto Clarkson St.
   - Destination will be on the right (300 feet) – 1242 Clarkson.

5. **GO TO 980 Grant Street** (the Colburn Hotel and Apartments).
   - Head south on Clarkson St toward E 10th Ave (.3 miles).
   - Turn right onto E 10th Ave (.3 mile).
   - Continue on to Grant St. - Park in Charlie Brown's lot or on the street at 10th and Grant.

6. **GO TO 3135 Marion** (Cassady ate breakfast naked in this house).
   - Take 11$^{th}$ Avenue to Downing.
   - Left on Downing (approximately 2.5 miles).
   - Right on 31$^{st}$ Avenue.
   - Left on Marion – the destination will be on the left.

7. **GO TO 2259 Gilpin** (an early Cassady sexual encounter happened here).
   - Head south on Marion St toward E 31st Ave (225 feet).
   - Turn left at the 1st cross street onto E 31st Ave (.3 miles).
   - Turn right onto Williams St (.7 miles).
   - Turn right onto E 23rd Ave (350 feet).
   - Turn left at the 1st cross street onto Gilpin St – destination is on the right.

# Reading

Cassady, Carolyn. *Off the Road. My Years With Cassady, Kerouac and Ginsberg*. Penguin Books, 1990.

Cassady, Neal. *The First Third*. City Lights Books, 1971.

Christopher, Tom. *Denver, Colorado. Neal Cassady and the Beat Generation*. tomchristopher.com.

Dinar, Joshua and Steen, Jeffrey. *Denver Then and Now*. Pavilion, 2002.

Ginsberg, Allen. *Collected Poems 1947 - 1997*. Harper Reprint, 2007.

*Kashner, Sam. When I Was Cool. My Life at the Jack Kerouac School*. Perennial, 2005.

Johnson, Joyce. *The Voice Is All: The Lonely Victory of Jack Kerouac*. Penguin Books, 2013.

Kopp, Zack. *The Denver Beat Scene. The Mile-High Legacy of Kerouac, Cassady and Ginsberg*. History Press, 2015.

Kerouac, Jack. *On the Road*. With an Introduction by Ann Charters. Penguin Books, 1991.

Kerouac, Jack. *Visions of Cody*. Penguin Books, 1993.

Morgan, Bill. *The Beat Atlas. A State by State Guide to the Beat Generation in America*. City Lights Books, 2011.

Moore, Dave, ed. *Neal Cassady Collected Letters, 1944 - 1967*. Introduction by Carolyn Cassady. Penguin Books, 2004.

Noel, Thomas J. *Buildings of Colorado*. Oxford University Press. 2002.

Noel, Thomas J. and Fielder, John. *Colorado 1870 - 2000. The History Behind The Images*. Westcliff, 2001.

Sandison, David and Vickers, David. *Neal Cassady: The Fast Life of a Beat Hero*. Chicago Review Press, 2006.

Made in the USA
Middletown, DE
21 December 2018